The first cup

Joke Book

Collection Compiled by Frank Wood

wK Books

Frank and Jenni would like to dedicate this book to all who appreciate the positive power of laughter and shared joy.

Introduction

First Cup with Jeremy was a martial arts morning show I worked on for about four years. During the time I was the show's producer, it was on Monday through Friday at 6:30 AM. The show was named *First Cup* because Jeremy did the show while having his first cup of coffee.

In the live chat during the show, many of the viewers gave updates on how they were doing. Many of the live viewers became like family to me. I still talk to most of them.

Over the years the show was many things. We celebrated unique holidays. Sometimes we discussed current events, but never politics. Other times it was part philosophy with thought-provoking quotes. Every Friday it was part comedy because that's the day Jeremy read the jokes I submitted.

The jokes on Funday Fridays were such a hit Jeremy suggested that I do a book of jokes. I often tell jokes daily, so it was a natural fit for me. I hope you have a good laugh!!

Enjoy.

~FW

The First Cup Joke Book

**Where can you find a
cowboy in the kitchen?**

On the range.

**Where can you find a
surfer in the kitchen?**

On the microwave.

**Why did the traffic
light turn red?**

You would, too, if you had to
change in the middle of the street like that.

Did you hear about the Vicks VapoRub truck that turned over on the highway?
It got Vicks VapoRub all over the highway!
But the good news is that there was
no congestion on I-71 for 6 hours.

The Elmer's Glue truck turned over on the highway.
They told motorists to stick
to the left lane.

Why did the girl put peanut butter on the road?
To go with the traffic jam.

I was going to tell you that joke about procrastination ...
but I think I better tell you later.

What are a twin's favorite fruit?
A pear.

Why was the tomato blushing?
It saw the salad dressing.

How do you fix a broken tomato?

With tomato paste.

The lettuce and the tomato got into a race. How did it go?

The lettuce went "ahead" while the tomato tried to "catch up."

I was going to tell you some produce jokes ...

but I plum forgot.

**Why does everyone want
to be friends with the orange?**

He has such a zest for life!

**What do they put on a
honeymoon salad?**

Lettuce alone.

**What do we say before
eating a salad?**

Lettuce pray.

Why did the banana quit sunbathing?

Because he was starting to peel.

What is a tree's favorite drink?

Root beer.

What did the grape say when it got stepped on?

Nothing. It just let out a little whine.

**Why were the baby
strawberries crying?**

Their parents were in a jam.

**What does a nosy
pepper do?**

It gets jalapeño
(all up in your) business.

**What does a farmer
use to mend his pants?**

A pumpkin patch.

**I was going to tell you
that joke about pizza ...**
but it's too cheesy.

**Why did the gardener
quit his job?**
His celery was too low.

**What did the skeleton
order at the restaurant?**
Ribs.

**Why couldn't the two
melons get married?**

They cantaloupe.

**What did the cheese lover
do with her new credit card?**

She went on a shopping brie!

**Why did the potato
cross the street?**

He saw a fork up ahead.

How do you make gold soup?
With 24 carrots.

**Why did the baker
quit baking donuts?**
He got sick of the whole thing.

**Did you hear about the
secretive baker?**
He kept his recipes on a
knead to know basis.

**Did you hear about
the rich baker?**

He made a lot of dough.

**What did baby corn
say to momma corn?**

Where's popcorn?

**Did you hear about the
popcorn that joined the army?**

They made him a colonel.

Why did everyone want to be friends with the mushroom?

He's such a fungi!!

What is a tree's favorite breakfast?

Oak-meal.

What does a pig use in the shower to clean himself?

Hog wash.

**Where do chess
players go shopping?**

The pawn shop.

**Did you hear about the
new gay version of poker?**

Queens are wild and

straights don't count.

**What's the most
dangerous part of a car?**

The nut behind the wheel.

**Why did the coffee
file a police report?**

He was mugged.

**I was going to tell you that joke
about the swimming pool ...**

but it's too watered down

to be any good.

**What's holding
up the moon?**

Moonbeams.

**Did you hear about the
restaurant on the moon?**
Well, the food's great
but there's no atmosphere.

**What dance did
the pilgrims do?**
The Plymouth Rock.

**What dance did
the containers do?**
The Can-Can.

**Why didn't the skeleton
go to the dance?**

He had nobody to dance with.

What do clouds wear?

Thunderwear.

**What did the paper
say to the pencil?**

Good point!

**What did the pen
say to the pencil?**

You look sharp.

**What did the pencil say
to the pencil sharpener?**

Quit going around in circles
and get to the point.

**Did I tell you the one
about the dull pencil?**

Oh well, there's no point.

**Why do you need a pencil
when you go to bed?**
To draw the curtains.

**Did I tell you that
joke about the roof?**
Never mind it's over your head.

**When is a door
not a door?**
When it's a jar.

Why did the spy go to bed?

He was undercover.

**Did you hear about the bed bugs
who fell in love?**

They were married in the spring.

**What do a dog and
a phone have in common?**

They both have collar (caller) ID.

Did you hear about how Santa only used 8 reindeer last year?

Comet stayed home to clean the sink.

What do you call someone who is afraid of Santa?

Claus-trophobic.

What is a snowman's favorite breakfast?

Frosted flakes!

**Why did the girl move
her bed in front of the fireplace?**

So she could sleep like a log.

**Who should you call in
case you injure your foot?**

A toe (tow) truck!

**Did you hear about
the award-winning farmer?**

He was outstanding in his field!

Did you hear about the guy who invented the door knocker?

He won the no-bell prize.

How many archeologists does it take to change a lightbulb?

Three — one to change the bulb and the other two to argue over the date of the old one.

How many doctors does it take to change a lightbulb?

It depends on what kind of insurance the bulb has.

How many construction workers does it take to change a lightbulb?

They're still working on it.

How many mystery writers does it take to change a lightbulb?

Two – one to put it almost all the way in and the second one to give it a surprise twist at the end.

How many psychiatrists does it take to change a lightbulb?

One, but the lightbulb has to really want to change.

How many economists does it take to change a lightbulb?

If the lightbulb needed changing
the market would have already taken
care of it. Just leave it alone.

How many baseball players does it take to change a lightbulb?

You can't use any. They're all too busy
arguing over the last call from the umpire.

What did the football coach say to the broken vending machine?

I want my quarter back.

**What runs up and down
the football field
but never moves?**

The fence.

**What's Irish and stays
out all night?**

Paddy O'Furniture.

**Why should you never
iron a four-leaf clover?**

You don't want to press your luck.

**Why should you never make
a bet with a leprechaun?**

They always come up a little short.

**What is an astronaut's
favorite part of a computer?**

The space bar.

**What makes a computer
so smart?**

It listens to its Motherboard.

**Why do golfers wear
two pairs of pants?**

In case they get a hole in one.

**What is a cat's favorite
part of golf?**

Birdies.

What do cats drive?

A Cadillac (cat-illac).

**Why is there a fence
around the cemetery?**

People are dying to get in.

**What has four legs
but one foot?**

A bed.

**What did one wall
say to the other?**

Let's meet at the corner.

**What do you call a deer
with no eyes?**

No-eye deer. (No idea).

**What do you call a deer
with no legs and no eyes?**

Still no-eye deer.

**What do you call a cow
with no legs?**

Ground beef.

**What do you call a cow
with only one legs?**

Lean beef.

**What is black and white
and red all over?**

A newspaper.

**How do you make
a tissue dance?**

You put a little boogie in it.

**Why did the belt
go to jail?**
For holding up a pair of pants.

**Why did the picture
go to jail?**
It was framed.

**They arrested the
energizer bunny.**
He was charged with battery.

**When do you need
ChapStick in the garden?**

When you plant the two-lips.

**What flowers make
the best friends?**

Rose buds.

**What kind of friends
does your mouth have?**

Taste buds.

**What did the tie
say to the hat?**

I'll hang around here.

You go on a head.

**What did the bra
say to the hat?**

You go on a head.

I'll give these two a lift.

**What did one oar say
to the other oar?**

Can I interest you in

a little row-mance?

**What did the French chef
give his wife for
Valentine's Day?**

A hug and a quiche.

**What do you call someone
without a body and
without a nose?**

Nobody knows!

**Why was the boy
excited to go to the cookout?**

He met the grill of his dreams.

**Did you hear about the
sale we had on glasses?**

It was quite the spectacle.

**Why should you never
lie to your cardiologist?**

Because he can detect a fib.

**What do you call a
ship twitching at the
bottom of the ocean?**

A nervous wreck.

Who cleans the ocean?
The mermaid.

**I just started a book
about anti-gravity.**
It's impossible to put down.

**How does NASA
organize a party?**
They planet.

**What did the father buffalo
say to his son when
he left for college?**

Bison.

Where do ghosts go fishing?

Lake Erie.

**Did you hear about the
new spoon they came out with?**

It's really stirring things up.

**Did you hear about the
new knife they came out with?**
It's on the cutting edge.

**Did you hear about
the new broom?**
It's sweeping the nation.

**What did the broom
say to the mop?**
I'm tired of people pushing us around.

**Why did the teacher
marry the janitor?**

He swept her right off her feet.

**I asked the librarian,
"Where can I find the book
Man: the Superior Sex?"**

She said, "I know that book. It's upstairs
in Science Fiction and Fantasy."

**What's the difference
between a US trust bond
and a man?**

The trust bond will eventually
fully mature whereas the man never will.

If you see the Apple Store getting robbed ...

does that make you an iWitness?

iPad+iBook+iPhone

=iBroke

Why does history keep repeating itself?

Because we weren't listening the first time.

**What's the difference
between fiction and nonfiction?**
Fiction has to be believable.

**Why did the students
eat their homework?**
The teacher told them it
would be a piece of cake.

**Where do you learn to
make ice cream at?**
Sundae school.

**What kind of chocolate
do they serve at the airport?**
Plane chocolate.

**At this point, the airlines
are so cash-strapped...**
they'll charge you for
your emotional baggage.

**Did you hear about
the pilot who was always
employed?**
He really knew how to land a job.

In Russia, they don't have Starbucks.

They have Czarbucks.

What three candies can you find in every high school?

Nerds, Smarties, and Dum-Dums.

When is a chair like a dress?

When it's sat in.

Why is 6 afraid of 7?

Because 7 8 9.

**Why can't you hear a
pterodactyl going
to the bathroom?**

Because the P is silent.

**What do you call
a running turkey?**

Fast food.

Why did they let the turkey join the band?

Because it had the drumsticks.

What happened to the turkey when he got into a fight?

He got the stuffing knocked out of him.

Why can't you take a turkey to church?

Because it will use fowl language.

**Why did the skeleton
not want to play football?**

His heart wasn't in it.

**What kind of tea do
football players drink?**

Penalty.

**Where do football
players dance?**

At the Foot Ball.

Why did Cinderella get kicked off the football team?

She kept running away from the ball.

Why did the football quit the team?

It was tired of getting kicked around.

Why did the ice cream truck break down?

Because of the Rocky Road.

How is ice cream as a girlfriend?

The sweetest.

Why is ice cream so bad at tennis?

They have a soft serve.

How did Reese eat her ice cream?

Witherspoon.

Why did the newspaper talk to the ice cream?

He was looking for the scoop.

Did you hear about the frozen dessert whose wife had a baby?

Now he's a popsicle.

What does an ice cream lawyer say?

You got served.

**What is ice cream's
favorite TV show?**

Game of Cones.

**Why do ice cream cones
always carry an umbrella?**

There's a chance of sprinkles.

**Did you hear about
the tree's birthday party?**

Things got pretty sappy!

**Why are birthdays good
for your health?**

Studies have shown that people
who have more birthdays actually live longer.

**How come you didn't
get me a birthday present?**

You did say I should surprise you, right?

**What's the fanciest kind
of birthday party you
can throw for a dog?**

A ball.

Why did the woman celebrate her birthday for only 30 seconds?

It was her 32nd birthday.

Why do all of my relatives keep reminding me how old I am on my birthday?

Because age is a relative thing.

What happens when a husband asks his wife for a Segway as his birthday present?

She just changes the topic.

**Why do tennis balls
whisper Happy Birthday
to each other?**

They don't want to make a racquet.

**Why do vampires not
want to become
investment bankers?**

They hate stakeholders.

Why are vampires bad at art?

They are only able to draw blood.

**Know why skeletons
are so calm?**

Because nothing gets under their skin.

**What do skeletons
order at a restaurant?**

Spare ribs.

**What's a skeleton's
favorite song?**

"Bad to the Bone."

**Why can't skeletons
play church music?**

Because they have no organs.

**What is a skeleton's
favorite instrument?**

A trom-bone.

**What do ghosts
like to wear?**

Boo-jeans.

Do you know why nobody wants to be friends with Dracula?

He's a real pain in the neck.

What did the egg do when it saw the frying pan?

It scrambled!

Why did it take the chicken so long to cross the road?

There was no eggs-press lane!

**What do you call a
mischievous egg?**

A practical yolker!

**Why did the egg regret
being in an omelet?**

It wasn't all it was cracked up to be!

**What was the motivational
egg speaker's slogan?**

Sunny side up!

Why did the rooster go to KFC?

He wanted to see the chicken strip

What do young chickens like to watch?

Chick flicks.

What do confused chickens lay?

Scrambled eggs.

Why didn't the chicken go to KFC?

It wasn't on her bucket list.

**Why did the man with
one hand cross the street?**

To get to the Second Hand Store.

**Why did the dinosaur
cross the road?**

Because chickens didn't exist yet.

Why did the chicken cross the road?

No one knows. But the road will have its vengeance.

Why did the penguin cross the road?

Because the chicken was busy.

Why did the cactus cross the road?

It was stuck to the chicken.

**I hope one day chickens
will be free to cross the road ...**
without having their motives questioned.

**What's the best day of the
week to go to the beach?**
SUN-day

**What did the beach
say to the wave?**
Long tide, no sea.

What do you say when the beach asks you to walk on it?

Shore!

Why is the beach friendly?

Because it waves!

How do men exercise at the beach?

While sucking in their stomach
every time they see a girl in a bikini.

Do fish go on vacation?

No, because they're always in school

What's the first card game played at the beach?

Go Fish!

Why do fish like to eat worms?

Because they get hooked on them.

**Where do sharks
go on vacation?**
Fin Land

Do you think the ocean is salty ...
because the beach never waves back?

**What is the strongest
animal at the beach?**
The mussels.

Where do sheep go on vacation?
To the Baaa-hamas!

**What do sheep wear
to the beach?**
A baa-kini.

**Why do fish not
like basketball?**
They don't like to get
too close to the net.

**How are fish and
music the same?**
They both have scales.

**Why kind of tan did
the pilgrims get at the beach?**
A puritan.

**Did you hear about the
man brought in by
the fashion police?**
They questioned him over his criminal ties.

Why is Princess Zelda the most fashionable person in Hyrule?

Because she's really Sheik.

Why did the mechanic have a disappointing fashion show?

There was no time to change attire.

We Want to Hear from You!

Reviews are an important part of how others find our books, and they help us create content you love. If you enjoyed this book, please visit this title's Amazon listing, Goodreads listing, or wherever you purchased your copy, and leave us a review. We will use your feedback to help create more content catered towards you, our loyal readers.

Thank you!

AVAILABLE FROM WHISTLEKICK BOOKS PUBLISHING

BY JEREMY LESNIAK

Non-Fiction

The Martial Artist's Handbook

12 Months to Health

How Not to Hold a Tournament

Stronger people Are Harder to Kill

Press Release Mastery

Simpler Social Media

Starting to Sell on Amazon

Fiction

Faith: The Katana Chronicles - Book One

*The Katana Chronicles - Book Two **COMING SOON!***

BY BARBARA W. MCCOY, MS

It's as Easy as Z to A: A Journey Through the Alphabet

BY JENNI SIU

The Origin of Master Hopkick: Beginnings

The Origin of Master Hopkick: Beginnings - Special Edition

The Origin of Master Hopkick: Beginnings - Instructor's Edition (w/ Chris Rickard)

The Origin of Master Hopkick: Lessons

*The Origin of Master Hopkick Book Three **COMING SOON!***

BY CHRIS RICKARD

The Instructor's Guide to Jenni Siu's The Origin of Master Hopkick: Beginnings - Mat Chat and Classroom Discussion Guide

BY JENNI NATHER

Modern Moms of Martial Arts: Volume One

COMPILED BY FRANK WOOD

The First Cup Joke Book

INSPIRED BY WHISTLEKICK MARTIAL ARTS RADIO

Collections

Celebrating Women in the Martial Arts
Legends of the Martial Arts
What Advice Would You Give Martial Artists 100 Years From Now?
A Journey Into the Badlands w/ Daniel Wu, Emily Beecham, and Sherman Augustus
The Karate Kid & Cobra Kai Collection
Restomp The Interviews w/ Master ken, Matt page, and Joseph Conway

One-on-One Interviews

Tony Blauer
Mr. Don "The Dragon" Wilson
Shihan Bas Rutten
Bill "superfoot" Wallace
Adrian Paul
Sensei Fumio Demura
Iain Abernethy
Five Faces of Kempo
Jhoon Rhee
Stephen Hayes
Nathan Porter

SEARCH US ON AMAZON FOR MORE TITLES!

wK Books

DON'T MISS OUR EVENTS!

ALL-IN WEEKEND

This 2-day martial arts event will be half training experience and half retreat. The cost of the event includes all of your training, your lodging, food, and an event shirt. All you have to do is show up, and we'll take care of the rest.

FREE TRAINING DAY

whistlekick's Free Training Day is exactly what the name says - one day of the year where martial artists come together to share and learn, all for free. There is no admission fee at this event, instructors are not paid, and whistlekick picks up the tab for the venue and any other logistical costs.

MARTIAL SUMMIT

Martial Summit is our vision for the future. A place where martial artists, from all over the world, of all systems and styles, come together to share. This 4-day event includes Free Training Day Northeast as well as the Never Settle Awards Banquet.

Follow the QR codes above or visit whistlekick.com and click on "For Individuals" to find all the latest info on our incredible events!

12 Months to Health

This book is designed to help you establish and reinforce 12 simple, inexpensive habits to achieve a healthier you in 12 months.

Available on Amazon!

"Mr. Lesniak has laid out a well-researched, simple, and gradual guide to real success in incorporating healthy habits into one's daily life. I look forward to sharing this with my patients as a partner in their journey toward better health."

— Joshua Singer, Licensed Acupuncturist at River Street Wellness, Montpelier, Vermont

"Setting just the right goal is hard to do, and starting with consistent, bite-sized, achievable goals is the way to achieve real change in your health."

— Irvin Eisenberg, Masters in Occupational Therapy, Structural Integrator and Owner of Resilience Occupational Therapy

"Our healthcare system, as it is built, right now, is largely not designed to help you until AFTER chronic disease strikes. Even preventative health endorsed by your doctor is left to the small choices you make daily, by yourself, well outside of the walls of the clinic."

— Joshua T. White, MD, MBA, Chief Medical Officer, Gifford Medical Center

"12 things that ANYONE can do that will make a vast difference to their life."

— Daniel Eagles

"A single focus for a month makes it much more likely that I will be able to make sustainable changes."

— StaciAnne KaeLeigh Grove

FREE whistlekick Flexibility Program!

Yes, I said FREE! This program is designed by and for martial artists with features you won't find in any other program, at any price. The Flexibility Program is rooted in the latest science, immensely effective, and different from what most of us were taught.

The FREE whistlekick 30-Day Challenge

The program is a FREE and COMPLETE standalone training program you can start at any time. It's designed to be done on its own, without other strength or conditioning programs. The daily workouts can be completed in about 10 minutes, require NO EQUIPMENT, and can be done in a small indoor space.

This program combines martial arts and fitness to get you the exact workout you need on that day. It helps you build momentum to gain more out of your time – with your health, fitness, training, and the rest of your life.

These are just a sample of the programs we offer!

Looking to increase your speed? How about your fighting endurance? Visit whistlekick.com to see how we are revolutionizing the way you train to improve not only your martial arts skills, but also your overall health.

Check out the collection of whistlekick Programs in the whistlekick Store today!

Want to Find More?

You may wish to check out one of our other titles, including *The Martial Artist's Handbook*, an introduction to topics related to practicing martial arts for fans and practitioners alike. Find the library of whistlekick books on Amazon by searching "whistlekick books" or ask your local bookstore owner or Library Director to stock our books on their shelves.

We Truly Appreciate You!

Thank you for supporting whistlekick Books. We invite you to visit us at whistlekick.com. While there, you will find links to check out our other books, our store, social media, how to leave us reviews, info on our other projects, and much more.

We are always open to your thoughts, questions, and suggestions. You may contact us anytime at books@whistlekick.com.

Thank you!

wK Books